LEECH

By JJI

Chapter 1

The world rots through the night; Thieves, drug dealers, pimps, and whores they all live for it. Draining the world; killers leeching off others flesh, rapists tearing apart lives, muggers stealing from the innocent, it was disgusting. At least, that's the way he saw things driving down the highway in a worn out green Neon.

Maxwell Amadeus Bernardo turned up the rock music that was playing on the car radio. He had average build wearing thin framed black glasses, blue jeans, and a black t-shirt. clean shaven and white teeth he had a cigarette between his right index and middle finger griped around the steering wheel. He sighed as he turned right onto an overpass, the sun setting as he did so. the station on the radio had been on repeat and he had heard singing about roses and their thorns three times now that he had been driving so long.

It had been a hot day and if his shirt had not been black it would be showing sweat stains. Those in the cars surrounding him happily unaware of what lye in the trunk of his car. He had it for a week now and had to get rid of it, or risk getting caught with it. Alas he tossed his cigarette butt out the car window and drove on the highway like it was any other day. when he reached a gas station he pulled into it, he was a little paranoid about the full service, if they smelled what was in the trunk of his car life would be over as he knew it. regardless he pulled in with a smile. "What can I do for you today Sir?" the man in a blue hat and overalls asked beside the car. Max had been driving all day and wasn't in the mood for conversation so he just forced a smile and said "fill her up" handing the man in blue eighty dollars and rolling up the window.

After the gas station he drove to the outskirts of the city where there was a forested campground, the kind of overgrown wooded area no one had thought about in years. An old rotten wood sign read "residence please sign in at the information cabins", but the sign was clearly decaying and the cabins to the west of the dirt parking lot he pulled into looked no better. As max got out of the car he lit another cigarette and paced to the trunk of the car. holding the cigarette in his mouth he unlocked the trunk with the key he had in his right hand and had to step back to throw up the contents of his stomach.

The trunk was filled with; a couple small boxes, a jerry can, some old magazines, and a large black sports bag. The bag was what was causing the horrid odor. It was what he had to get rid of. Normally he would get rid of this kind of thing in a day or two, he had never waited a whole week before. The problem was the smell it made it detectable. nevertheless he grabbed the bag and walked off into the dark woods with a flashlight on his keychain.

In the midst of the woods, just off the beaten trail was a large hole in the ground which max had dug a week before. He put the bag down beside it and put the cigarette out on the bottom of his shoe. He put the cigarette but in his pocket, he couldn't leave a trace. As he opened the bag and pulled out the mangled corpse of the six year old girl he coughed at the stench. It was a week's worth of decay. He tossed the corpse into the hole and began covering it with the mound of dirt adjacent. after he was done he walked away with the empty bag and forced smile on his face. At

last he was rid of it, now he could go home.
He walked through the woods and back to
his car. He got in the car and put the key in
the ignition.

*

In a theater room
packed with people in row seats Jeremy
Fredric Eloh stood in line on the left side of
the stage third from the stairs to the stage.
The bearded man on stage was giving a
speech on how outstanding all the
graduates were. Jeremy, his hair combed
into a good boy, was in suit and tie, as were
the other students in line with him. Jeremy
straightened his black tie as the man on
stage behind a podium said "and now the
graduates," with a large smile. As the two
in front of him were called up on to the
stage in turn he couldn't wait to receive his
own certificate. He looked to the crowd

where is mother and younger sister were sitting front row, his mother holding a camera.

"and now" the bearded man onstage said with enthusiasm "Mr. Jeremy F. Eloh" turning his gaze on the left of the stage as Jeremy stepped onto the stage. He strode across to the podium center stage. he took the certificate from the bearded man and they shook hands. Jeremy then walked of the right side of the stage and made his way around the crowd to a large door. this was the highlight of his career, graduating law school was the first step to joining the RCMP and fulfilling his dreams of being a spy. The door opened to a large hall where tables had been set up with food and assorted beverages for an after party to the graduation. The chandelier gave a classic appeal to the hall and it was clear by the people sitting at the tables eating that the party had begun already.

Jeremy made his way into the hall and to the nearest table and sat down next to a fellow graduate. He too was wearing a suit and tie but his hair was a lighter shade of auburn than Jeremy's. He turned his head looking at Jeremy as he sat down with a happy "Congrats on the graduation Jer!" while placing down a chicken wing on the plate in front of him. "Yeah same to you," Jeremy replied with a smile. The number of people in the hall grew as they ate and eventually Jeremy's mother and younger sister came striding across the hall toward him. It was his law school graduation so they probably expected a hug and to give him a gift. Jeremy placed down a chicken wing on his plate and turned toward his family. "Hey mom, Hey Jess how is it going." Jeremy said, wiping his fingers in a napkin, "get a good picture?" His younger sister Jessica held out a little white envelope with glitter decoration on it. "Congratulations" the little eight year old girl said.

He took the envelope with a thankful hug and opened it casually. They did this at his high school graduation too, so he couldn't act like he didn't expect it. as he pulled out the card he smiled as five one hundred dollar bills fell into his hand, catching them just shy of the chicken wing sauce on the table. "Thanks" He sighed with a grin. "A hundred of that is from my lemonade stand over last summer" Jessica smiled. As the party went on his family left and his stomach grew full so he got up, said goodbye to everyone that was still there, and left through a large door. he went down some stone stairs and across a parking lot to a red sports car. As he got in his car he pulled a keychain out of his

breast pocket and closed the car door. he
sighed and put the key in the ignition.

*

Chapter 2

There was a pause in his words as he pulled down the map. It rolled smoothly out of the cylinder on the ceiling. The map was old and worn, it could easily be seen that thumbtacks had been pushed thro it and the detailed image of north america was faced with a laminated RCMP crest in the top right corner for a compus. As he turned to face the dozen men and women in suit and tie seated at the long mahogany table behind him Jeremy cleared his throat. "Now, we're here to discuss the possibility of a very agile serial killer," Jeremy stated as he looked to the others, "At first the missing girls were seen as isolated incidences, but now with the numbers growing we have a possible serial killer targeting children." Jeremy took five tacks out of a small box on the table next to him. He had been doing this kind of thing for over a year now and was beginning to do this one with a lack of enthusiasm. "We have fifteen missing girls, from five school districts, all under the age of ten, over the last two and a half years." Jeremy stuck the tacks in the map all centered around southern ontario canada. "That means six girls a year, which means Ontario is due for another missing child."

Jeremy placed his hands on the table and sighed, "Any thoughts so far?" A man sitting near the front leaned into the table and said "Perhaps increase security around the school zones in the area?" looking at Jeremy through his thin framed black glasses. "Yes Bernardo," Jeremy reassured as he stood up straight, "we are doing all we can in that regard." It was true; they had sent flyers to the families of the students, they even had police cruisers on the usual routes the students would take to and from school.

At the end of the meeting it was four pm and Jeremy's shift ended at seven, so he had just enough time to do some of that week's paper work. As Jeremy passed through the halls of the RCMP headquarters he was handed a three inch three ring binder of papers by a short ginger haired man in a suit. "Thanks O'brien" Jeremy smirked and continued walking. He passed by an office with a plaque on the door reading "Maxwell A. Bernardo" in gold lettering. He took a clipboard of some notes out of the binder and slipped it through the mail slot below the plaque. He continued walking to the office next to Bernardo's, with a similar plaque reading Jeremy F. Eloh, and opened the door.

In his office Jeremy had; a large desk, a computer, a book case of binders and a nice hard wood floor. His desk was scattered with notebooks and two 1 inch binders. There was no window but there was a landscape painting of a mountain range on the wall and that was enough of a view in Jeremy's opinion. He sighed as he sat in the leather chair behind his desk and placed his new binder on the reflective mahogany finish. His desk was scattered with his life's work and then some. He always had a lot of paperwork, even on the weekends he had to take some home with him. He picked up a black composition notebook and opened it. A pen he had been using as a bookmark slid out into his left hand and he began recording the meeting details.

The small digital clock on his desk passed through 3 hours before he finally closed his notebooks and binders with a sigh of relief. He got up and opened a drawer in the desk which creaked with a sharp pitch. He had always meant to call maintenance for the desk, but never cared enough to pick up the phone. He pulled a pair of black sunglasses with blue tinted lenses out of the drawer and closed it one crack at a time. All the missing children in ontario and all the time they lost on the case to paperwork, it was a lot to handle and they days just dragged on forever. He put the sunglasses in his suit jacket breast pocket and crossed the room to the door. Hitting a light switch left of the door he left the room, leaving the luminescent green clock on his desk to be the only light in the room.

*

       Thin framed black glasses, short brown hair, and clean shaven; Maxwell A. Bernardo sat in an arm chair in his large well furnished living room watching Television. The man on the television was giving the latest news broadcast for the region of waterloo ontario Canada. It had been a long time since Max had watched the news, he usually just read the front page of the paper at work before meetings. "Two missing girls in two weeks time, are these cases connected in some way? The RCMP certainly think so, stay tuned for more after this." The television cut to commercial but it was drowned out by loud stomping noises from upstairs. Max sighed and looked at the ceiling. He grabbed the remote that was on the couch next to him and turned the television off as he stood up. He tossed the remote back onto the couch and walked toward a staircase adjacent the living room.

Picking up a blood stained baseball bat at the bottom of the stairs he cleared his throat. All the time he spent beating this one and still she insisted on stomping and screaming. As he got to the top of the stairs the stomping became barely audible crying and screaming. Max opened the door, to the right, at the top of the stairs. It took a lot of effort to keep his little hobby quiet. He had kidnaped the girl a week ago and she still kept fighting for her freedom. He rested the bat on his left shoulder as he opened the door and walked into the room.

The only light in the room was a beam of sunlight coming in through the window at the far side of the what would be master bedroom of the house. As max closed the door behind him the was a clanking of chains within the shadows. She was the oldest yet at age 15 in a green t-shirt and blue jeans, chained to the wall by a steel collar which looked hand made. "Let me out of here you bastard!" she screamed while laying on the floor. Max slowly paced into the light above the girl.

"P-please j-just let me go" she whispered with tears in her eyes as she curled into fetal position. "Shut up, you are never getting out of here bitch." max said calmly as he swung the bat down at the girl's back and broke it with a loud snap. He was able to be so casual having done this so many times. She shivered and cried, she was to used to the pain to scream now. "A-alright, I'll shut up" she cried as she crawled to the wall her chain was bolted to and sat there hugging her legs crying. Max slowly left the room and closed the door leaving the only light in the room that beam of sunlight from the window, soon to fade away.

*

Chapter 3

In a calm common suburb, In the middle of the afternoon on a sunny day. With well attended landscaping and beautiful white brick houses, Talon street seemed like a paradise where you could find a smiling neighbour around every corner. As a black SUV was driving down talon street it slowed and pulled over to the curb. Its tinted windows shone images of the surrounding street.

When two men in suits, One with short brown hair and thin framed black glasses, and the other with slightly longer auburn hair They walked walked up the curb and down a nicely tiled walkway. "They should be here this time right" Max asked Jeremy. They had already tried to meet with Mr. and Mrs. Thompson three times now. The last three times they had been out doing various errands. "Yes," Jeremy said with an air of sarcasm, "I called them half an hour ago to confirm."

When they reached fourteen Talon street Max knocked on the door, and both reached to their hip for their identification. Jeremy rung the doorbell on the right hand side of the door. The sound of a small dog barking inside the home and a woman's voice telling it to shush signaled that they were in fact home. With the sound of the dog fading deeper inside the house footsteps could also be heard behind the door. As the door opened a women in her mid thirties stood just inside. "Can I help you?" she questioned as max and Jeremy held up their Identification. She was wearing a flower covered blue dress and had long brown hair. "Oh, come on in, we'll talk in the living room."

As she walked down a hallway inside and into a room to the right Max and Jeremy stepped into the house. There was a staircase immediately to the left of the door and a long hallway leading straight to a kitchen with an opening on the right hand side of the hall opening to a large fully furnished living room. As they entered the living room a man on a leather sofa took a remote and turned off the television on seeing them. "Good afternoon Mr. and Mrs. Thompson." Jeremy said as he sat in a leather arm chair in the nicely carpeted room. Max sat in another chair as Mrs. Thompson sat on the sofa with her husband. "We know it's not a happy situation but we need all the information we can get." Maxwell continued for him.

This case was three days in so the chances of finding her alive were very slim. Sarah Thompson was

kidnaped at churchill park cambridge
Ontario Canada. After the interview they
were going to the park to look for other
witnesses, not that it was very hopeful
searching three days later. "We already told
the police, we don't know where she is and
her friend said a tall man in glasses
grabbed her and put her in the trunk of his
car" Mrs Thompson said with a hesitant
depressed tone. "Well that rules out the
teenage runaway theory" Jeremy said with
a questioning look at Max.

                        "Well do you
know where we can find this friend?" Max
asked with a sigh. This was bad if they got
a sketch max might as well turn himself in.
"Her name is Jen, she lives down the street,
number twenty two." Mr. Thompson said in
his persistent frown. "Well we have another
stop before the park," Max sighed, he was
nervous if she gave his description and his
licence plate he would have to run from the

RCMP. "yes, we have to go talk to Jen" Max thought to himself. The two of them thanked Mr and Mrs. Thompson for their time and made their way out of the house while a sound of the small dog echoed from upstairs. "I think we should just call a sketch artist to go to Jen's house, let's get to the park." Jeremy said closing the door behind them and stepping into the sunlight

*

Searching the park revealed nothing they didn't already know. It was not like the one who did it would have stuck around and it had already been three days so witnesses were nowhere to be seen. The park was crowded so it was difficult to investigate anyway. "Alright let's call it a day and hope the team got a good sketch out of this Jen girl." Jeremy said exhausted driving down the highway in the black SUV. "My place or yours first? " Max asked glaring out the window at the setting sun, one of them had to take the SUV back to headquarters in the morning. "I'll drop you off and take the SUV back tomorrow, you seem tired." Jeremy replied. Max was nervous though you wouldn't be able to tell his training at the RCMP made him good under pressure. "Yeah, alright." max said leaning back in his seat.

As they pulled into the driveway of Maxwell's the sun had set and it was dark but for the moonlight surrounding. Max stepped out of the car saying "thanks." Jeremy nodded and max shut the car door. He walked up to his front door as Jeremy pulled out and drove away. Stepping inside he closed the door. "Fuck," he said to himself in an angry tone. When he got to his kitchen he picked up a plate that was on the counter smashing it off the wall. He quickly opened a drawer in the counter and pulled out a black handled butcher knife. He left the kitchen with it at a brisk pace.

There was quiet stomping noises coming from upstairs, he had to get rid of her, get out of town, and so he walked up the staircase in his living room and down the hallway. The stomping was louder when one was upstairs and audible crying could be heard. As Max opened the door and stepped into the room she begged "please, y-you don't have to do this." her clothes now stained with blood and her emaciated body badly bruised she has sprawled out on the floor crying. "Shut up!" Max grunted. The chain bolting her to the wall by the window clanked as she stood. "Please" she cried, the knife in maxwell's hand glistening in the moonlight coming through the window. "I said" he raised his voice, "Shut up!" he walked slowly with light hysteric laughter. He

grabbed the fifteen year old girl and began
sawing into her throat with the butcher
knife she struggled for a moment but once
Max sawed through her neck vertebrae and
she lost enough blood she went limp and
pale. Max then dropped her lifeless body to
the ground and walked to the corner of the
room to pick up a black sports bag. He then
crudely shoved the dead girl into the sports
bag. He left the room with it leaving a
puddle of blood glistening in the moonlight.

*

The hours were
ticking by, the highway was lit only by his
headlights and the signs used to direct
traffic. Max had the sports bag on his lap as
he drove his neon. He rolled down the
window and floored the gas pedal shoving
the sports bag out the window in the middle
of the highway. Now that he had gotten rid
of the girl he just had to make it down the
highway. He had a house in manitoba for

this kind of screw up. The trip there was going to be costly on gas and with the RCMP on his tail he had to hurry. He had it planned so well. He had a hundred thousand dollars in cash he had in boxes in the trunk of his car to get by until he changed his identity. Or at least that was the plan.

*

The clock was ticking past 8 pm in the meeting room of the RCMP headquarters. Jeremy was sitting at the head of the table facing nine other men and two women, all in suit and tie. The mahogany reflective finish of the table was covered in paperwork and pens the only empty seat was that of maxwell. the apprehensive air of the room was getting even more depressing as they all started to realize that Max was not coming back. It was enough that max did not show up to the meeting on the sketch when it looked just like him.

"Ok now, there is a serial killer and he has been under our nose the whole time as one of our own." Jeremy started to the sad faces around the table for the loss of a trusted friend. "We will send a local swat team to raid his home and find as much evidence as possible." Jeremy then looked down the table to a blond haired women and questioned, "and where is the updated report on the possible drug cartel throughout Canada Diana?" she passed down the table a file folder "right here, and you'll be happy to hear we have planted a successful mole." Jeremy smiled at this and took the folder "thank you, at least something good happened today." jeremy looked up from the folder and to man on his left, "What is more, do you have that report on your firearm Marshal?" The man leaned back in his chair and ran his hand through his hair, "It's not due until next week, I'm still working on it." Jeremy smirked "At any rate we have a lot to do and barely enough time to do it all, everyone has to pay as close attention to this Bernardo case as possible.

*

Chapter 4

The raid of maxwell's house only improved the case against him. The puddles of blood throughout the house matched the blood type of Sarah Thompson, That and the corps was found on the highway nearly beheaded. They couldn't even have an open casket at her funeral because of the badly abused body. Though they had no leads on where Max was going but they knew he had to be a least out of the province because the body was found on the overpass just before the Trans-Canada Highway.

Sarah Tompson alone was twentyfour years to life in prison but with the likelihood that the cases in recent years were connected Maxwell was guilty of much more than her murder driving down the highway. He slowed down and pulled into a parking lot of a motel just off the side of the highway. The old asphalt crunched under the tires of the worn green neon. Max parked and got out of his car slowly. The light coming off the cars passing nearby and off the cheap looking motel were dim and the moon was the brightest of them.

Cold, was the word the man behind the front desk in the main checking in portion of the motel said as max entered through the door with a chime. "oh, it's getting to be around that time of year again.." Max replied with a light chuckle. He walked up to the desk with a smirk and pulled his wallet out of his pocket "how much is a room for tonight?" the man, wearing a red checkered uniform behind the desk, took a key off the wall behind him and put it on the desk opening the cash register. "fifty a night but considering the time twenty will do." max pulled a green twenty dollar note out of his wallet and gave it to the man behind the desk.

*

　　　Sunlight was shining through the window of the elementary school classroom, books lined shelves on the walls and the couple dozen children sitting at desks were all looking through a text book. A twelve year old girl was reading a passage aloud as a elderly woman was writing the main points of the text on a blackboard in chalk. "In the spring of 1605, under Samuel de Champlain, the new St. Croix settlement was moved to Port Royal" the little girl read aloud, " today's Annapolis Royal, Nova Scotia. And In 1608, Champlain founded what is now Quebec City, which would become one of the earliest permanent settlement and the capital of New France." The elderly woman turned from the board and smirked. "Yes, thank you Jessica, Now all of you write that down and study over the weekend, we will be having a test on monday.

After the young students all finished their note the bell of the school rang. The children all went to the back of the classroom and opened a cupboard containing many backpacks. Each student grabbed their bag in turn and left the classroom. As Jessica made her way out the front door of the school a blue car honked its horn to signal her. She walked over and got in the car. "Hi mom" she smiled as she put on her seatbelt and put her bright green backpack on the seat beside her, "I have a test on Monday, can you help me study over the weekend?" The woman in the front seat smiled and started driving down the street. "Sure Jess, what is the test on?" she replied and turned a corner away from the school. "History, colonization of Canada." Jessica said as she stared out the window.

As they drove through town they Talked about Jessica's day at school and a little about the history of canada. When they arrived at home they got out of the car. There was a red sports car parked out front of their house and Jeremy stepped out of it as His mother and sister approached. His sister ran up to him and gave him a hug, his mother smiled as she walked up to the two of them. "Shouldn't you be at work?" Jessica smiled as she let go of him. "It's my day off" Jeremy smirked, "Turns out I actually get one once in a wial."

The three of them went into the house and sat in the living room. "Just thought I would drop by and give you fair warning we are probably going to send you two to a safe house in winnipeg," His mother's face dropped "It's only until we capture this guy who threatened to come after you two" Jeremy sighed. "When is this going to happen" Jeremy's mother asked. He stood up and sighed "it'll be in a few weeks and it's only until we catch maxwell, Jess's school work will be brought to her and once we know you're safe, we will bring you back here." Jeremy gave his sister one last hug and said he would see them again soon.as he got back in his car he took his green key chain and put the key in the ignition.

*

Chapter 5

Sunlight was shining through the window of the motel window to room six. Max awoke at eight in the morning in his cheap motel room, it wasn't due to the alarm clock, it was more due to the noise of the traffic outside. He got up put on his glasses and leather jacket to cover up his blood stained shirt. He had to get to Steinbach Manitoba, He had bought a house there that he never told anyone about in case of this exact situation, so he opened to room door and stepped out into the parking lot. He returned his key to the front desk, which had a new cashier then last night, and got back to his car. In his car he sat for a moment and sighed while gripping the steering wheel.

He turned on the police scanner that was installed under the radio and sat to listen for a few minutes. The voices were static and muffled but max was used to hearing it after so many years. From what he could get out of it the RCMP had set up roadblocks at either end of the ontario border along the TransCanada highway, and they had his vehicle description. After lighting a cigarette he began to drive down the highway. The number of cars around him was getting larger as the day went on. He pulled of the highway and drove around northern Ontario for about an hour until he arrived at a border to Manitoba that was a good distance from the highway. He pulled through slowly and no one seemed to notice him. So he got through without a problem, if it hadn't been for his scanner he might just have been caught that day. He gave a sigh of relief as he made it through the border. He continued south through Manitoba until he reached The town of

Steinbach. He owned a house there but He
never told anyone about it, it wasn't even
on the power grid.

As he pulled into the
driveway of a lone house down country
roads he Threw a cigarette butt out the
window of his car. The house was old and
worn and the lawn was overgrown but at
least he could lay low here. He got out of his
car and walked up to the old home. As he
opened the door He took his Jacket of and
hung it on a hook next to the door while
closing and locking the door. It was night by
the time he got there and since he had no
electricity it was dark. He stood and let his
eyes adjust to the new venue. There was a
generator in the basement and once max
had it up and running, well, let there be
light. It was not a bad place for him to be at
the moment though, since years of sitting
there, some of the furniture was bug
infested. It took a little cleaning but max

eventually was able to make himself comfortable. Since the water was running from a well nearby he was able to shower and have a change of clothes, he threw the blood stained clothing in the grabadge. And fell asleep in a queen size bed on the second floor of the house, master bedroom.

*

Tony was by far The richest of the men in the Cartel, he was making money off twelve different drugs, the main one being Heroine. He was also a gambler bringing in about three million dollars canadian a year, mostly cash but his many bank accounts were full as well. Recently a runner up in the Cartel, James Carter, was working alongside him in cocaine sales. Little did Tony know James was the mole for the RCMP and he was getting close to having enough evidence to arrest Tony.

Sitting in a large armchair in a victorian style room with a chandelier on the ceiling Tony was talking to James. "So, how many kilos this month in manitoba? Three hundred as usual?" Tony raised his eyebrow, glaring at James with a stern look. "I regret to inform you that Manitoba sales have gone down hill, it seems the addicts have switched to methamphetamine Hydrochloride." Tony leaned back in his chair and stroked his goatee. He sighed and leaned back forwards after a moment. "That loses us five hundred thousand dollars a year... I will throw heroin at manitoba at a discount price for the first month and raise it then, make more money with it than with meth." Tony leaned back again. "have you ever done any work with heroin before James?" He asked with a smirk, "it's quite a lot of money. Eighty dollars a gram, how would you like to help me out?" James just smirked back

at Tony and nodded his head. Just then the
wire James was wearing made a wizzing
sound and Tony Jumped up and pulled out
a desert eagle 40 cal. Hand gun. James's
body was never found and without his
recording the RCMP had nothing to go on.
Alas as tony would say, "That is what
happens to rats."

      Meanwhile in Manitoba Max
was walking through town looking for a
drug dealer. He was not an addict by any
means but he had to make money fast and
drugs did that. He was walking downtown
and came across an alley so he walked
through. There was a man with a pipe half
across the alley and as max approached he
quickly hid his pipe. Max smirked "You
know where I can find some of that?" The
man gave a sigh of relief and pulled his pipe
back out, "yeah, I can take you to Chris... he
sells it to me, you know it's meth right?"
Max stood there talking with the man for

about five minutes and gained a little trust
by having some smoke, he had alcohol
before but it was nothing like meth.

*

      With James missing
Diana's team was struck with heartache
and the only other way to make a come
back from it was to plant another mole in
the cartel but no one was as good a spy as
Carter, he had graduated law school at the
age of fifteen on a scholarship he earned in
the middle of high school. They had to
choose someone as good or better then him
or they would never get to Tony again,
especially now that he new they were on to
his cartel.

      The meeting room had the
usual crowd, minus Bernardo, and
Jeremy had the map pulled down again.
"O.K. Carter is missing and we can assume

he is most likely dead," Jeremy was saying, "this cartel and the bernardo case go hand in hand, due to the trafficking charges Max had in high school, he will most likely turn to trafficking for money again given these circumstances." Jeremy sat at the head of the table and opened a three ring binder in front of him. Diana leaned forward into the table and cleared her throat. "We have another mole, Chris Radford, But he is nowhere near talking to Tony Randel." Jeremy looked up from his binder. "Well we just have to wait for him to get in deeper to bust the cartel, where is he located now?" Diana leaned back "Manitoba, Steinbach Manitoba."

*

Chapter 6

On seeing Chris Radford's face Max recognized him and quickly got out of his sight. He knew that Chris had recognized him as well. It was to late now for regret and it was only a matter of time before the RCMP heard he was in Steinbach. All he could do was hope they would think he left Steinbach when he was seen, which was very likely. Max was at the local library and he seen a woman in her mid-twenties early thirties maybe. They got talking and using his charm and wit he convinced her to go back to his place with him.

Once they got there they walked up to the house and max held the door for her. As she stepped in she had a smile on her face, the last one she would ever have. Max quickly broke her neck and paralyzed her after closing the door. He dragged her by her hair into the living room and stood over her giving a smirk. She wheezed a light "what the hell" as she coughed up blood. Max walked calmly to the kitchen and grabbed a fillet knife. As he paced slowly back to the living room he gave light maniacal hints of laughter "kill her, rip out her digestive system, let her starve to death" he thought out loud. Nearly going blind in a psychotic break he eviscerated the woman, staining the carpet of the living room with blood.

When he was finished he took what was left of the corps and burned it in the back yard. The smell was awful but he had his fill of his little addiction so he was content. He even roasted marshmallows over her burning corps and made smores. They tasted good but had the stench of burnt flesh. The very next morning Max took the burnt remains and threw them in the road down town and drove away glad to be rid of them. The gas tank was empty, time to fill her up again.

*

Diana was walking through the hall of the RCMP headquarters holding a three inch binder full of paper. As she entered her office she turned on the light Unlike Jeremy her office had a window, and a dove was perched on the sill.it whistled lightly through the open window as Diana sat behind her desk in a leather office chair.When she reached the section labled Tony Randel she paused for a moment and sighed out of annoyance. She grabbed a pen and began taking notes.

As Time passed the light outside dimmed and the dove made a nest. She looked at a clock that was on her desk and realized what time it was. She shut the binder and stood up. She left her office and turned off the light leaving a moonlit dove to be the only sight in the room.

Just when you think the day is done and she is going home a red light flashed from the ceiling and an alarm sounded "warning, warning, anthrax alert, anthrax alert room 7A, room 7A." Diana ran out of the building as fast as she could and once she was in the underground garage she pressed a button on her keychain and her car unlocked and she drove home.

*

Jessica and her mother were in a moving truck driving down the trans canada highway. Jess was staring out the passenger seat window with blank look on her face. Her mother driving adjusted the rearview mirror and sighed. "Jess what do you want for your birthday?" Jess looked to her mother away from the window. It was lightly snowing outside in mid January and the highway was surprisingly less busy than usual. "I don't know, something I guess" she replied. The usual response she gave to such questions. She was content with her christmas gift every year, this year a new cellphone, and she just wanted to go home.

Suddenly an eighteen wheeler truck swerved on some ice and slid into their lane. A log it had been hauling flew through the windshield and right into her mother's face. Blood flew out of her jugular vein onto Jessica's face as she screamed. The truck continued sliding just missing the moving truck but taking out its side view mirror. Jessica stuttered a whispered "m- m- mom" in a tearful tone and shakingly took out her cellphone from her pocket.

When the ambulance arrived her mother was already bled dry but they took her back to the hospital anyway due to jessica's pleading. The nearest hospital was in manitoba and due to the police escort jessica was taken to the safehouse by a police officer who stayed with her until her father could be discharged from the army to look after her.

*

Chapter 7

In april the snow had gone and it was raining outside. Jessica was staring out the window of the house her and her father had been living in for four months now. Her father walked into her bedroom and she turned to look at him. "Happy birthday Jess" he said calmly. The smirk she gave was the closest thing to a smile she had gave since her mother passed. "Not really" she sighed with a depressed tone. Her father sighed and looked at the floor, "I miss her too." He left a small green gift wrapped gift with a card on her bedside table and muttered a "j-just plain old birthday than." When her father left the room with a sigh she stared back out her bedroom window while rain drops rolled down the glass as a tear down her face.

Later on that evening she opened her gift, a video dvd of her last 13 birthdays, the card read "Jess, over the years there was good times it wasn't all bad, and your mother would have been so proud of you, for all you have been through you still manage to see the best in life. I know it's hard to celebrate anything right now since she is not here but I miss her too you're not the only one and if you ever want to talk I'm still here. Love Dad." she placed the card down on the bedside table and put the dvd in the computer in the corner of her bedroom. As she watched and every time she seen her mother smile it made her cry, not so much out of sorrow but out of closer.

Jessica walked down the stairs outside her bedroom and went into the kitchen. As she opened the fridge The doorbell rang through the house and there was a knock at the door. She went to the door but her father was already there opening it. Jeremy's face was the first thing to make her smile in months she ran to the doorway and hugged him with a huge smile on her face. He stepped into the house as she let go of him and looked at his father, "hey Dad," Jeremy sighed.

*

Chris Radford Met
Tony Randel on the first of June. It had
only been for a moment but he knew he
would be able to get closer eventually. The
Meth he had been selling had now turned to
heroine and the knife he had carried was
now a gun. Not much could be said about
his moral after that, he always seemed
upbeat until that point, but love is not a
victory march.
As Tony stood next to
him on the elevator of the old apartment
ment building they chose to meet in he
smirked and lightly chuckled `So how is the
business these days. Chris gave a forced
smirk back `it's not as booming as meth but
the money is more lately.` As they stepped
off of the elevator and walked down a
hallway a door at the end of the hall
opened, and a man in a pastel suit stepped
out. The man in pastel walked up to them
and Tony smirked `Help Chris load a kilo of
down into the trunk of the car outside.

Chris waited outside the door while Tony and The man in pastel went inside the room. The man in pastel came back out of the room with a large box on a dolly. They went back down the elevator and out to Chris`car. Chris shook the man`s hand and got into his car. The man put the box in the trunk of his blue sunfire and walked back into the building. Chris drove away after staring at his steering wheel a few seconds.

*

Max was walking down the street in Winnipeg Manitoba. He had left steinbeck in a rush and was now living in his car. At this point he was beginning to consider turning himself in. the charges were only building at this point and if he pleaded guilty he would still be in jail the rest of his life. He was only going to be in winnipeg a few weeks so that the police in steinbeck could search all they wanted and not find him, then he would go back to his house and not have to live in his car, this time he would avoid killing anyone.

He walked into a cafe on the corner of the street and ordered a coffee. He was given the coffee black and was told to go to the table in the middle of the cafe where there was; cream, sugar, milk, and sweetener. So he could make his coffee exactly the way he wanted to. The jazz music playing on low volume in the cafe made the setting. It added a real cafe feel to the place. As Max sat down at a table with his coffee he notice a wanted poster on the wall with his face on it. "Shit" he thought to himself. At least he had grown a beard since the picture so he was barely recognizable. Still it made him nervous not being able to tell if anyone recognized him.

After his coffee he left the cafe and began walking back to his car, which was near a park at the other end of the street but by the time he got halfway there he noticed a police car parked next to it. He was running the plates for sure and there was no doubt that he could not go back for his car. He turned around and walked in the other direction hoping no one would notice him in his nervous psychotic state. Once out of site from the park he hijacked a car stopped at a red light, and headed back to steinbeck.

*

Chapter 8

The blue pontiac Max had stolen in winnipeg was a bit of an upgrade from his old neon, but still old enough to not have a trace on it. As he was driving down The highway to Steinbeck There was very little traffic. Halfway down the highway Max seen something that frightened him, Jeremy's car in his rear view mirror. Max floored the gas and the car screeched and stalled. Jeremy crashed into the back of maxwell's stolen pontiac.

As Jeremy got out of his car and walked up to the blue pontiac that was a front him The engine of the vehicle tried to start three times. He quickened his pace to the driver side window and for a moment time stood still. Jeremy, after realizing the situation took his gun from his waist sheath shaking at the wrists. A year ago pointing his gun at max was one of the last things he thought he would ever have to do. Now, on the other hand, he knew it had to be done.

Max quickly scrambled out the passenger side door and took cover on the opposite side of the car than Jeremy.

Max looked at Jeremy through the car windows. "Jer, I was going to turn myself in" Jeremy lowered his gun and replied "Then why are you hiding behind the car," Max stood tall and looked eye level with Jeremy over the car, "I think you know the answer to that riddle Jer, so put it away I'll go with you quietly." Jeremy put his gun back in his sheath and raised his hands. Max walked around the the car and stood next to Jeremy with his hands behind his back. Jeremy took handcuffs from his waist and cuffed Max walking back to his red car with him.

*

Chapter 9

Life is short, and its only a matter of time until your six feet under, in an urn, or the odd man eaten by a shark or a bear. In other words in Tony's mind ash to ash was gun powder to gun powder. The drug cartel he had been running since he was in high school was now a multi billion dollar industry. Despite the money to pay anyone off he was still at risk of prison no bail and all because of addiction.

Chris Radford was now one of the most trusted men in Tony's main circle of dealers, and also a mole for the RCMP. The time was drawing near to arrest Tony for conspiracy of drug trafficking across North America. Standing in an elevator Tony and Chris were both dressed in finely tailored suits. "So, hows business in Manitoba?" Tony gazed questioningly at him, Chris Gazed back
and with a stern face said: "fine, just fine." The elevator doors opened.

A women in a dress blue
with scarlet trim was standing outside the
elevator to greet them. "hello Tony who is
this, you didn't say anything about a guest,
I need to order more food." Tony smirked
and sighed, "Matilda, he is just leaving we
Just needed to talk for a minuet no need for
extra lunch."

*

In a court room the serial
killer Maxwell Amadaeous Bernardo was
handcuffed sitting to the right side of the
room, stood up and was escorted to the
seats at the front of the room. The Judge
cleared his throat and began "Maxwell
Amadaeous Bernardo, you stand accused of
murder in the first degree how do you plea."
Max cleared his throat and a woman in the
seats behind him shouted "He killed my
daughter, she was only fifteen."
     The Judge cried order, and
the woman sat down shut up and began to
cry quietly. Max looked around behind

himself at every one seated and the jury before saying "Oh I've done so much more than that." the judge looked at him and said "and just what have you done"

Max gave the location of twelve bodies, all children except for the one women he had evicerated. When they found them they threw max into a high security penitentiary for life no bail unless good behaviour for twenty years.

*

RCMP officer Jeremy F. Eloh was at his fathers house. Jeremy his father and younger sister Jessica were sitting at the dinning room table eating dinner and as they finished Jeremy stood up first with a smirk: "I have to get home, There is a report to file on Maxwell." His father stood up picked up his empty plate and walked over to the sink: "I still can't believe he got away with it for so long, twelve bodies in three years, that is four a year."

Jessica walked with Jeremy to the door. She smiled and said: "thanks for staying this weekend Jeremy, I know its hard to have a family get together without Mom." Jeremy look at her and sighed: "Yeah, I know." She gave him a hug and he walked to the driveway got in his car and began to drive home.

Stopped at a gas station his cell phone rang from the glove box of his red topless sports car. As he grabbed the phone he couldn't help but think something was wrong. He finished pumping the gas as he answered the phone: "hey Chief, what has happened now," Jeremy dropped the phone. As he picked it back up he was still in shock at the news of Maxwell's escape from prison.

*

Chapter 10

Max was driving the streets of Steinbeck Manitoba Canada in a blue Honda civic wearing a police uniform. He suffocated a guard at the prison, hid the body in his cell, and walked out the front door in his uniform. He was now heading to his old house in Steinbeck to hide. He just had to make it there without having a cop run the plates of his new car.

As he pulled into his drive way the gravel crunched under the car tiers. He stepped out of the stolen Honda he snickered manically. Walking up to the house he cleared his throat and sighed. He opened the door to a darkly lit home, The house had a generator in the basement so it wasn't on the electrical grid and he had a safe haven there. After turning on the generator and cleaning up a little he made himself coffee and sat in the upstairs

bedroom in his own clothes from one of the
closets in the master bedroom
                    The next morning
Maxwell's escape was all over the news. He
had taken the plates off the car he stole and
replaced them with fake plates he made
years before the whole fugitive thing. He
drove into town and picked up groceries at
a local super market. a radio next to the
cashier giving a news broadcast "Maxwell
Amadeus Bernardo, a serial killer, has
escaped from a prison near Steinbeck
Manitoba." Max looked at the radio and
then at the cashier "I guess I'm locking my
doors tonight." max sighed to the cashier.
The cashier smirked and bagged the food
max had bought.

*

            Jeremy was in his office at
the RCMP headquarters in his suit and tie.
The digital clock on the desk was flashing
green luminescent 8:30PM. The notebooks
and binders spread out on his desk were lit

only by a small desk lamp. He massaged his left temple and sighed: "Max... why?"

The clock alarm went off at 9:00pm and Jeremy closed and locked his office door as he left for the night. He headed down the hall and took an elevator to an under ground parking lot. He got in his red sports car and pulled out of his spot. Driving out of the parking lot he shifted gears and smirked as he leaned back in his seat.

Once home he loosened his tie while getting out of his car in the driveway. The moon was full that night and as he got to the door of his house his cell phone wrung in his pocket. He took his cell phone and answered it quickly: "I am off duty can this wait until morning?" Jeremy stopped abruptly, "arrested Tony, what about his wife.. Matilda"

*

Maxwell sat in his home at a desk. Pen in hand he had small lined paper on the desk. He began to write;

Dear Jeremy,

sad to hear about your mother, I hope you don't take it personally that I deceived you for all those years. This ache in the pit of my stomach is unlike anything I could explain in one letter I want to turn my self in but this voice inside compels me to continue this path. Somehow I feel you will be the one to catch me but before you do lets make this a game of tag, its my turn to play the cat to your mouse. Only question in my mind is when the wise say ash to ash, which one of us will be under ground.

With what time has left

- Max A Bernardo

Max grabbed an envelope that was on the desk and licked its glue put the letter inside and sealed it. He addressed it RCMP Headquarters Ontario Canada, N7Y-8I7 and put Jeremy F. Eloh in the centre. He stood up envelope in hand and left the room.

*

Chapter 11

In an interrogation room Tony and Diana were sitting across from one another at a table. Tony was giving a blank expression toward her and she just opened a file folder.: "Tony, we have video evidence from an undercover officer and a large amount of both meth amphetamine hydro- chloride and Morphine seized by our drug Crimes department that says you are behind a huge Cartel across Canada we plan on charging you with conspiracy, Money laundering cultivation and distribution of a lot of drugs and weapons, and murder in the first Degree of James our missing informant.

Tony smirked and leaned back in his chair: "all good things must come to an end." He ran his right hand through his medium length hair and sighed: "You win, what do you want to know?" Diana smirked and closed the folder: "names, Locations,

and your testimony in court against your
runner ups. We can guarantee you get bail
set at two million maximum

  Tony scoffed: "Testimony..." he
stared at the ceiling and sighed.: "alright I
need a cigarette, you get me a cigarette and
you got it... and a lighter too, ASAP." Diana
stood up and left the room and returned a
minute later with a pack of cigarettes and a
zipo's lighter placed them in front of Tony
on the table and sat back down.

       *

  Jeremy was just getting in his
office when a small envelope was slid into
the mail slot on his door by a short ginger
haired man in a suit. Jeremy looked over
his shoulder and took it to his desk leaving
his office door ajar and saying: "Thanks
O'brian," The ginger haired man in his
green suit outside the door said: "top of the
morning," clapped his heels and ran away
down the hallway shimmering.

Jeremy opened The letter with a sigh. One glimpse at it and he dropped it on his desk and grabbed a nearby wireless phone: "we have a problem," After about five minutes a tall man in a grey suit walked into Jeremy's office. : "what is the problem Jeremy" the man said with a questioning glare: "Maxwell, he just sent me a letter, I don't think it's a prank, he threatens me in it.

Jeremy and the man took the letter to the fingerprinting process and confirmed it was Maxwell's prints. That was enough to give concern to Jeremy and He ordered to send his sister and father to the safe house in manitoba with an RCMP escort

*

Jessica was walking out the front door of her school with her back pack on her back. Her father was waiting at the street out front with a RCMP in uniform officer she stopped afront them and sighed:

"why is he here Dad, I thought all that was over now..." She looked at the ground all sad like.

the Three of them got in a large black SUV. Her father looked at her from the front passenger side seat and sighed: "I'm sorry but Jeremy's case opened again Max escaped from prison a little while ago and threatened him therefore us.

As they pulled into the driveway of the safehouse Jessica looked out the window at a squirrel crawling up the tree in the front yard and smirked: "at least I get to see something I like when I look out the window." her father got out of the car first along with the RCMP officer. She got out as her father opened the rear care door and smiled: "at least you can still think positive thoughts."

*

to be continued

Made in the USA
Middletown, DE
23 August 2021